World of Reptiles

Copperheads

by Matt Doeden

Consultants:
The Staff of Reptile Gardens
Rapid City, South Dakota

Capstone *press*

Mankato, Minnesota

Bridgestone Books are published by Capstone Press,
151 Good Counsel Drive, P.O. Box 669, Mankato, Minnesota 56002.
www.capstonepress.com

Library of Congress Cataloging-in-Publication Data
Doeden, Matt.
  Copperheads / by Matt Doeden.
    p. cm.—(Bridgestone books. World of Reptiles)
  Includes bibliographical references and index.
  ISBN 0-7368-3731-0 (hardcover)
  1. Copperhead—Juvenile literature. I. Title. II. Series: Bridgestone books. World of Reptiles.
  QL666.O69 D63 2005
  597.96'3—dc22   2004014479

Summary: Discusses copperhead snakes, including what they look like and what they eat, as well as
reproduction, young, and dangers to the snake.

Editorial Credits
Heather Adamson, editor; Enoch Peterson, book designer; Ted Williams, cover designer;
  Erin Scott, illustrator; Jo Miller, photo researcher; Scott Thoms, photo editor

Photo Credits
Allen Blake Sheldon, 6
Bruce Coleman Inc/Joe McDonald, 20
Corbis/Joe McDonald, 12
Corel, 1
McDonald Wildlife Photography/Joe McDonald, 4
Peter Arnold, 18
Tom Stack & Associates/Joe & Carol McDonald, cover; Ryan C. Taylor, 16
Unicorn Stock Photos/Jack Milchanowski, 10

1 2 3 4 5 6 10 09 08 07 06 05

Table of Contents

Copperheads

Copperhead snakes get their name from the color of their heads. The red-brown color is the same color as a copper penny.

Copperheads are reptiles. All reptiles are **cold-blooded**. Reptiles also have scales and grow from eggs.

Copperheads are pit vipers. Pit vipers have small holes, or pits, below their eyes. The pits sense heat and help copperheads hunt for **prey**. Rattlesnakes and cottonmouth snakes are also pit vipers.

◀ Copperheads get their name from the red-brown color of their heads.

What Copperheads Look Like

Copperheads have thick, heavy bodies. Adults are usually 2 to 3 feet (0.6 to 0.9 meter) long. Many copperheads have a scale pattern of brown bands. These markings wrap around the snake's body.

Copperheads have flat, triangle-shaped heads. The wider part of the head holds **venom**. Sharp fangs fold down inside the copperhead's mouth. Copperheads use the fangs to poison prey.

◄ Copperheads store venom in pouches on the sides of their heads. The pouches give the head a triangle shape.

Copperheads Range Map

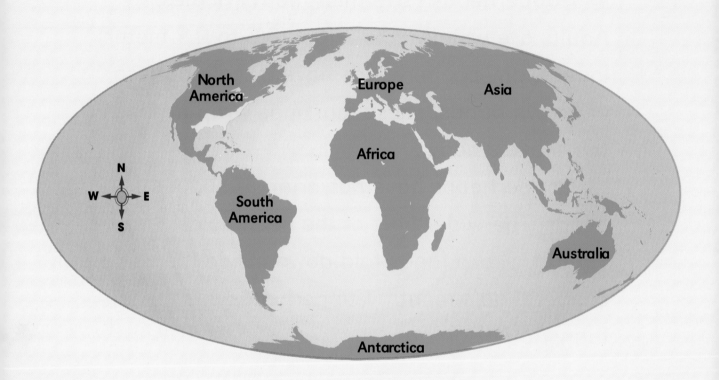

☐ Where Copperheads Live

Copperheads in the World

Most copperheads live in woodlands in the southeastern United States. Copperheads do live in other places though. Northern copperheads live as far north as Massachusetts. Trans-pecos copperheads live as far west as Texas. Broad-banded copperheads live as far south as Mexico.

◀ Five different kinds of copperheads live in eastern North America.

Copperhead Habitats

Copperheads usually live near rivers or ponds. They often make their homes in places with many plants. They may also live under fallen tree logs or under rocks.

During winter, copperheads **hibernate** in dens with other snakes. Copperheads often use dens in rocky hillsides where the sun can warm them. Copperheads use the same den year after year.

◄ Copperhead markings allow them to blend in with dirt and sticks on the ground.

What Copperheads Eat

Copperheads eat small animals, such as rats and mice. They also eat birds, lizards, frogs, and insects.

Copperheads are hunters. When a copperhead strikes its prey, it shoots venom through its fangs. A copperhead's venom causes the prey to bleed inside its body. Copperheads swallow their prey headfirst.

◄ A copperhead swallows its prey headfirst. This way, the the prey's legs fold neatly and do not get stuck.

Life Cycle of a Copperhead

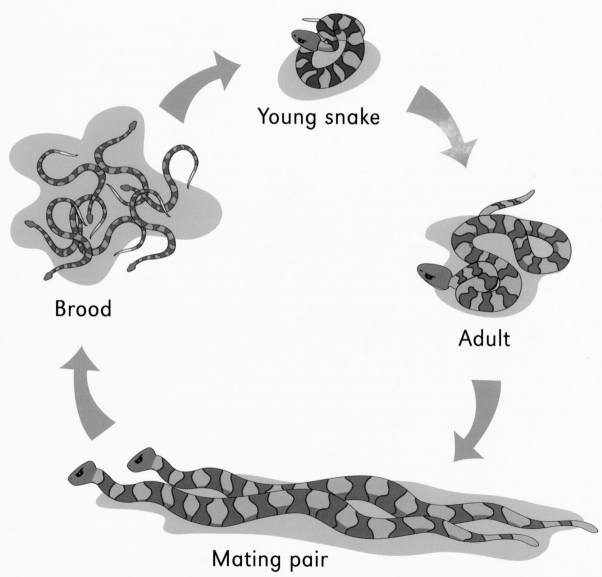

Young snake

Adult

Mating pair

Brood

Producing Young

Copperheads **mate** in late spring or early fall. Females only mate with strong males. Males sometimes fight each other to show a female they are strong.

Young copperheads grow in eggs inside the mother's body. The young are born live in thin sacs. Copperheads are always born in spring. Four to eight copperheads are born at one time. A group of young snakes is called a brood.

Growing Up

Copperheads are born ready to hunt and live on their own. Young copperheads have yellow tails that look like worms. Copperheads use their tails to trick prey to come close.

Copperheads grow quickly. Their skin becomes very tight as they grow. A new skin grows underneath the old skin. They shed their old skin, or **molt**, several times each year. Few copperheads in the wild live to be more than eight years old.

◄ A young copperhead wiggles its yellow tail like a worm to get prey to come close.

Dangers to Copperheads

Copperheads have some **predators**. Roadrunners, hawks, eagles, and other birds kill young copperheads. Large king snakes sometimes eat copperheads.

People can be a danger to copperheads. People build houses and roads in places where copperheads live. People also hike and climb near copperhead homes. Copperheads try to avoid people. Most people try to avoid copperheads too.

◄ A roadrunner catches a young copperhead for its next meal.

Amazing Facts about Copperheads

- Copperheads have bitten more people in the United States than any other snake. A bite needs treatment, but it doesn't usually kill a person.
- Some copperheads try to make a sound like a rattlesnake's rattle. They drag their tails back and forth across dry leaves or rocks to scare animals or people.
- Copperheads can grow new fangs. When a copperhead loses a fang, a new fang slides into place. A copperhead may use dozens of fangs during its life.

◀ A copperhead shows its fangs. Copperhead fangs are hollow. They sometimes break or get stuck in prey.

Glossary

cold-blooded (KOHLD-BLUHD-id)—having a body temperature that is the same as the surroundings; all reptiles are cold-blooded.

hibernate (HYE-bur-nate)—to spend winter in a deep sleep

mate (MATE)—to join together to produce young

molt (MOHLT)—to shed an outer layer of skin; copperheads molt several times as they grow.

predator (PED-uh-tur)—an animal that hunts another animal for food

prey (PRAY)—an animal that is hunted for food

venom (VEN-uhm)—a poisonous liquid made by some snakes; snakes inject venom into prey through hollow fangs.

Read More

Feldman, Heather. *Copperheads.* The Really Wild Life of Snakes. New York: PowerKids Press, 2004.

Murray, Julie. *Copperheads.* Animal Kingdom. Edina, Minn.: Abdo, 2003.

Internet Sites

FactHound offers a safe, fun way to find Internet sites related to this book. All of the sites on FactHound have been researched by our staff.

Here's how:
1. Visit *www.facthound.com*
2. Type in this special code **0736837310** for age-appropriate sites. Or enter a search word related to this book for a more general search.
3. Click on the **Fetch It** button.

FactHound will fetch the best sites for you!

Index